First Favorites

COMPREHENSION GUIDE
VOLUME TWO

Comprehension Questions
by Laurie Detweiler

Illustration and Design
by Ned Bustard

veritas
PRESS

Copyright © 2002 Veritas Press
www.VeritasPress.com
ISBN 978-1-930710-63-4

Printed in the United States of America.

First Favorites Comprehension Guide
Contents

FIRST FAVORITES COMPREHENSION GUIDE
How to Use this Guide

What is *First Favorites?* It is a collection of literature guides to assist beginning readers to enjoy and comprehend a book. Once children learn how to decode words they need to learn how to engage the materials. They need to learn how to comprehend what they are reading. So how do we do this?

The books may be read in any order, but we have placed them in order based on difficulty. Generally, we spend three to four days per book. With chapter books such as *Frog and Toad are Friends* you may need five to seven days. Children generally will read the book twice during this time. They should be reading the books aloud with you. You should help them to decode unfamiliar words. Be sure to let children sound out the words, rather than just giving them the pronunciation. Teach them to read with expression, which includes following the punctuation.

The comprehension questions and activities are there to help children focus on particular portions of the text and to help you assess their understanding of it. The children should be allowed to refer back to the text if needed. Although the answers in the guide are provided in incomplete sentences, you should expect the student to answer in complete sentences.

Example:

Question: What did Mr. Putter eat in the mornings?

Answer: Mr. Putter ate English muffins.

The art activities are meant to bring the text alive. Children always retain more when they work with the material. Handwriting exercises will provide students practice sentences to rehearse manuscript writing.

Below you will see four icons. Each will help you identify how to use each worksheet.

 COMPREHENSION QUESTIONS, WRITING EXERCISES

 COMPREHENSION ACTIVITIES, WRITING EXERCISES

 ART ACTIVITIES

 HANDWRITING EXERCISES

Enjoy! Curl up with a good book and read the day away. It is our desire that your students will become life long readers and look back on these years with great delight.

Sincerely,

Marlin Detweiler
Laurie Detweiler

Madeline

by Ludwig Bemelmans

Name: _____

Circle the words that rhyme with each word.

MICE
rain   ice   fire

HOURS
flowers   plants   vines

LIGHT
right   wrong   maybe

DRANK
car   crank   bed

BED
yellow   red   blue

HABIT
rabbit   horse   cat

CRY
dry   wet   sun

LIGHT
summer   night   morning

Name: _____

Finish the picture to show what was on the old house in Paris.

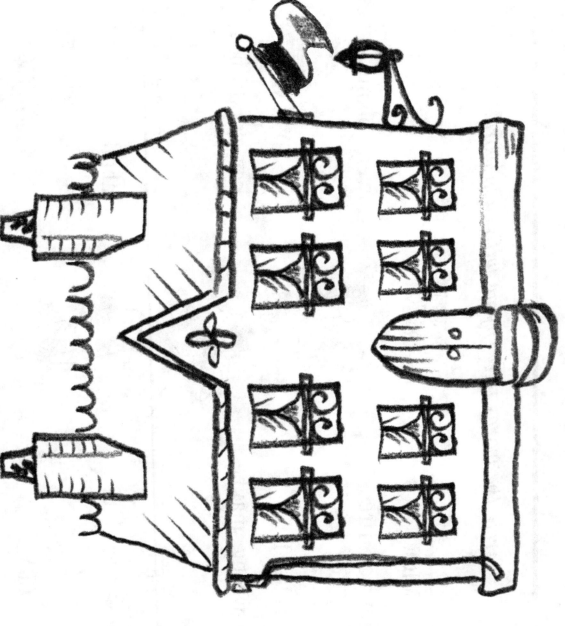

Name:

In the story the twelve little girls did many things in two straight lines. Draw three of the things they did.

Name: _____

Fill in the crossword by completing the sentences below.

Across

2. The smallest girl was _____ .

3. The little girls lived in two _____ lines.

Down

1. Madeline cried and cried because her _____ hurt.

4. In an old house in Paris lived _____ girls.

5. Madeline had a _____ on her stomach.

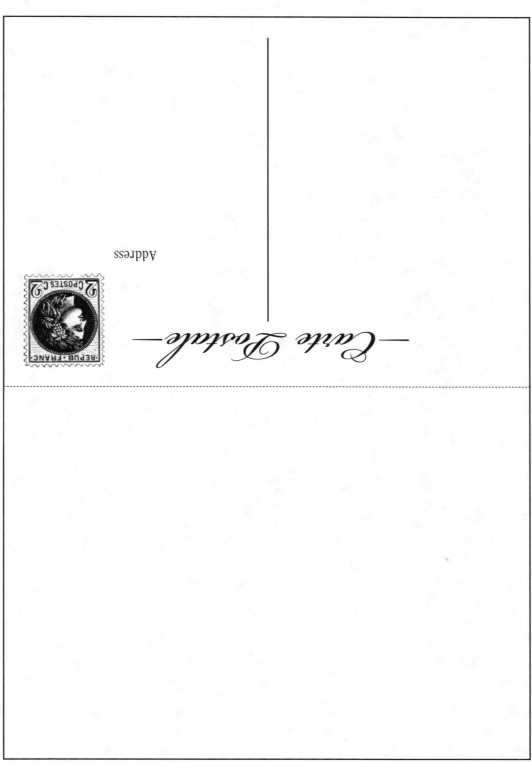

Carte Postale

Address

Draw a picture on the blank side of the card (the dotted line should be the top of your illustration) then cut it out and fold it over. On the address side write a message describing something that occurred in the book, as if you were one of Madeline's friends.

Name:

In your best handwriting copy the sentence below.

They left the house at half past nine

in two straight lines in rain or shine

—the smallest one was Madeline.

Nate the Great

Nate the Great
and the Lost List

by Marjorie Weinman Sharmat

Name:

Pancakes for Nate

Ingredients

2 cups buttermilk *(add more as required for proper consistency)*
2 eggs, not beaten
2 tablespoons melted butter
1 teaspoon baking soda
1 teaspoon sugar
1/4 teaspoon salt
1-1/4 cups unbleached flour
1-1/2 teaspoons of baking powder
Optional: sliced banana, chopped pecans, chocolate chips, or blueberries

Directions

Stir together buttermilk, eggs, and butter. Sift together flour, baking powder, baking soda, sugar and salt. Combine all ingredients. Stir gently, then ladle onto a pre-heated, buttered frying pan. When pancake begins to bubble you may want to add optional ingredients before flipping. Turn when golden brown. Cook other side to golden brown also. Serve with heated maple syrup. Makes: 12 to 14 pancakes.

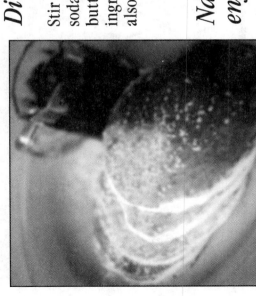

Nate the Great enjoyed pancakes! We hope you will enjoy these as you read these stories.

Name: _____

Answer the questions below using complete sentences.

What was Nate the Great?

What did Nate the Great have for breakfast?

Name: _____

☐

Answer the questions below using complete sentences.

What did Annie want Nate the Great to find?

Describe Annie.

Name: _____

Answer the questions below using complete sentences.

Describe the missing picture.

_____
_____
_____
_____
_____
_____
_____

What color did Annie like?

_____
_____
_____
_____
_____
_____

Name: _____

Answer the questions below using complete sentences.

Describe Fang.

_____
_____
_____
_____
_____
_____
_____
_____

Why did Nate dig in Annie's yard?

_____
_____
_____
_____
_____
_____
_____
_____

Name: _____

Answer the questions below using complete sentences.

Describe Rosamond.

What did Rosamond want Nate the Great to find?

Name: _____

Answer the question below using a complete sentence.

Where did Nate find Annie's picture?

How did Nate the Great know that
Harry had painted over Annie's picture?

Name: _____

Color in tiles below in such a way that the tiles left white make a picture like the one in Rosamond's home (you may want to look at the picture in the book).

Photocopy the picture below onto card stock. Then paint it using a primary color (red, yellow or blue). While the paint is still wet, paint over the picture using another primary color. What is the final color of your picture?

Name: _____

Answer the questions below using complete sentences.

What was the name of Nate's dog?

What case did Nate the Great take?

Name: _____

Answer the questions below using complete sentences.

Why did Rosamond look strange and white?

_____

Why did Nate the Great think Fang took the grocery list?

_____

Name:

Answer the questions below using complete sentences.

How did Nate make Fang drop the piece of paper?

What paper did Fang have in his mouth?

Name: _____

Answer the question below using a complete sentence.

Where did Rosamond get her

cat pancake recipe?

Where did Nate the Great find

the grocery list?

Name: _____

Be a detective! Find out who made each statement in the story.

I am a busy detective. _____

I am Nate the Great's dog. _____

I drew a map. _____

I made cat pancakes. _____

I tried to eat the map. _____

I thought the grocery list was a recipe. _____

I found the missing grocery list. _____

Name: _____

Maps help us to know where things are. In the space below draw a map of your street or schoolyard like Nate did. Here are some symbols you may want to use.

house

trees

road

water

swings

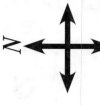
N
S

Name: _____

In your best handwriting, copy the sentences below.

My name is Nate the Great. I am a detective.

My name is Nate the Great and I like pancakes.

MISS NELSON IS MISSING!

BY HARRY ALLARD

Name: _____

Name: _____

Answer the questions below using complete sentences.

Describe Miss Viola Swamp?

Where had Miss Nelson gone?

Name:

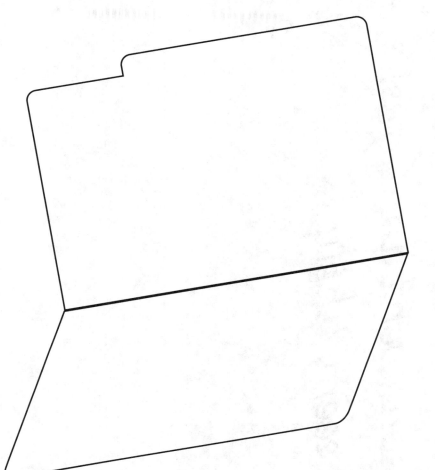

Detective McSmogg is putting together the case of the missing teacher.
Draw a line from ONLY the items involved in the mystery to this case folder.

Name: _____

In your best handwriting, copy the sentence below.

Maybe Miss Nelson went to Mars!

But that didn't seem likely.

THE BIGGEST BEAR

by Lynd Ward

Name: _____

Answer the questions below using complete sentences.

Where did Johnny Orchard live?

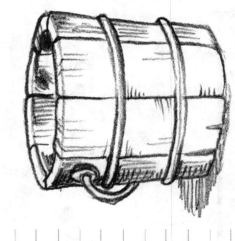

Define humiliated: (use a dictionary)

Name: _____

Answer the questions below using complete sentences.

Why did Johnny always feel
humiliated as he walked to the store?

How did Johnny get caught
in the bear trap?

Name: _____

*Illustrate in the four ovals
what Johnny's bear
liked to eat.*

Name: _____

Color the bear eating honey.

Name: _____

Match these statements with the character who said them.
There may be more than one quote per person.

He will have a fine place
to live, and all he wants
to eat. And you can come
and see him whenever
you want to.

It really upsets me when
your bear goes through
my kitchen shelves.

Humph. I suppose you
know what a bear
likes to eat.

I like to eat mash, apples,
pancakes and
maple sugar.

GRANDFATHER

ORCHARD

JOHNNY

MEN FROM THE ZOO

MR. McLEON AND
MR. McCARROL

JOHNNY'S MOTHER

JOHNNY'S BEAR

That bear of Johnny's is a
trial and tribulation to
the whole valley.

Better a bear in the
orchard than an
orchard in the bear.

If I ever see a bear I'll
shoot him so fast he won't
know what bit him.
And we'll have the biggest
bearskin in the
whole valley.

And I'll always bring
him maple sugar.

Name: _____

Did This Happen?

Read each sentence. If it occurred in the story, make a smiley face. ☺
If it did not occur, make a sad face. ☹

○ Johnny Orchard lived in a big city.

○ *Johnny's grandfather planted orange trees in the orchard.*

○ Johnny was so proud of the bearskin nailed on the barn door.

○ *Johnny fed a bear cub maple sugar.*

○ Johnny's bear cub liked to eat mash, apples, pancakes and maple sugar.

○ *Mr. McLeon and Mr. McCarrol loved Johnny's bear cub. They wanted him to stay around forever.*

○ Johnny tried to take his bear back to the woods, but he kept coming back.

○ *Johnny took his cub in a boat to Gull's Island. The bear lived there for the rest of his life.*

○ Johnny and his bear became prisoners in a trap made of logs.

○ *Johnny's bear went to live in a zoo, where Johnny could visit him.*

Name: _____

In your best handwriting, copy the sentence below.

The bear liked the milk that
was meant for the calves.

A New Coat for Anna

BY HARRIET ZIEFERT

Name: _____

Answer the questions below using complete sentences.

Why was Anna's mother
unable to buy her a new coat?

_____

_____

_____

_____

What idea did Mother have
to get Anna a new coat?

_____

_____

Draw a coat on Anna to show what her coat looked like.

Name: _____

Answer the questions below using complete sentences.

What was the first thing Anna's
mother said they needed for a new coat?

_____

_____

_____

_____

How did Anna and her mother color
the wool red?

_____

_____

Name: _____

Answer the questions below using complete sentences.

The tailor said he would be happy to make Anna a new coat. What was the first thing he needed to do?

_____

_____

_____

What did Anna want to do to celebrate Christmas?

_____

_____

Name: _____

Answer the question below using a complete sentence.

What did Anna's mother make for the celebration?

Name: _____

During the Second World War people had very little money. One way they were able to get what they needed was to trade items that they had, for items they wanted. *Match the people and their goods on the left to what Mother traded for on the right.*

Farmer and Wool	Teapot
Spinner and Yarn	Lamp
Weaver and Cloth	Gold Watch
Tailor and Coat	Garnet Necklace

Name: _____

Draw a line from the bubble to the one who said what is in the bubble.

WHEN THE WAR IS OVER, I WILL GET YOU A NICE NEW COAT.

A LAMP. THAT'S JUST WHAT I NEED. I WILL SPIN YOUR WOOL INTO YARN.

I WILL TRADE YOU WOOL FOR YOUR GOLD WATCH.

BAA! BAA!

THANK YOU FOR THE WOOL, SHEEP. DO YOU LIKE MY PRETTY NEW COAT?

WHAT A PRETTY NECKLACE. I WILL BE HAPPY TO WEAVE YOUR YARN.

THAT'S A PRETTY TEAPOT. I'D BE HAPPY TO MAKE YOU A NEW COAT, BUT FIRST I NEED TO TAKE YOUR MEASUREMENTS.

Name: _____

Cut out the picture of the sheep. Glue cottonballs onto it and attach clothespins for the legs. Then color the boxes on this page, cut them out and tape them together to form the paper chains Anna put on the sheep at Christmastime.

Name: _____

In your best handwriting copy the sentence below.

Winter had come and Anna needed

a new coat.

Hans Christian Andersen

THE EMPEROR'S NEW CLOTHES

Name: _____

A timeline shows us the order in which events occurred.

After reading the book, fill in the blanks to finish out the timeline. Then cut the timeline out and glue together onto construction paper.

Two men came to the town where the emperor lived.

The men told the emperor

_____
_____
_____
_____

The emperor said, "I must have

_____
_____
_____
_____

The emperor sent his two chief ministers to see the cloth being woven.

The men sat at the looms and pretended to weave.

The emperor gave the men
_____
_____
_____
_____

The two men pretended to work hard on the cloth. They pretended to sew the emperor a new _____ .

The emperor looked at the loom and thought
_____
_____
_____
_____

The chief ministers told the emperor that the cloth was
_____
_____
_____
_____

Name: _____

The emperor looked in the mirror and said
_____
_____
_____

The emperor took off his clothes and the two men pretended
_____
_____
_____

The morning of the parade the emperor came to try on his new cothes.

In the street people were waiting to see the big parade. When they saw the emperor they said
_____
_____
_____

The emperor and the noblemen marched out of the palace.

Two noblemen were supposed to hold up the ends of the emperor's new cape. They felt around on the floor and pretended to
_____
_____

Name: _____

A little child saw him
and said

_____
_____
_____
_____

The emperor heard
what was said and
realized that he did
not have clothes on.

The emperor thought
"The parade must
go on so he

_____
_____
_____
_____

The two noblemen
walked behind him,
holding up the ends of
the new royal cape that
was not there.

Name: _____

Choose from from the following list to find the synonym
for each word and write that word by its synonym.

king | sew | incredible | pretty | cloak | aristocrat | castle | radiate

emperor _____

shine _____

palace _____

beautiful _____

weave _____

cape _____

amazing _____

nobleman _____

Name: _____

Help the emperor by making a new coat for
him using crayons or colored pencils to create
a beautiful design in the area provided below.

Name: _____

In your best handwriting, copy the sentence below.

There was once an emperor who loved new clothes. He spent all of his money on clothes.

STONE SOUP

by Marcia Brown

Name:

When you follow a recipe in a cookbook you end up with luscious food to eat. When you read this book you can see that the author used a "recipe" to write the book. Have fun filling out the recipe card below.

RECIPE: *Stone Soup*

INGREDIENTS: _____ , three _____ , salt, pepper, _____ ,
cabbage, _____ , potatoes, barley,
and _____ . and a village of gullible _____ .

DIRECTIONS: Take three wise _____ and add three
_____ . Heat a _____ of water and add three
_____ . Sprinkle in liberal amounts of out-loud musings about
how good the soup *could* be if salt, pepper, carrots, _____ ,
beef, potatoes, barley, and _____ were available to include.
Watch the soup carefully as the villagers simmer with excitement.
_____ to drink — garnished with dancing.
Serve hot with _____

SERVING SIZE: *One Village + 3*

Name: _____

Underline the nouns. Circle the adjectives. Place an "X" over the verbs.

Three soldiers trudged down a road.

A large pot was filled with water and three stones.

The peasants added carrots, salt, pepper, cabbage, beef, potatoes, barley and milk to the soup.

They ate and drank and ate and drank.

Name: _____

Vegetable  Stone Soup

Ingredients:
4 cups water
3 washed stones tied up in cheese cloth
2 lbs. beef cubes
2 tbsp. cooking oil
3 carrots diced
1/2 large cabbage, chopped
3 large potatoes, diced
1/2 cup barley
1 cup milk

Directions:
Place the three clean stones into the middle of a piece of cheese cloth and tie cloth. Place stones in cheese cloth bag into a crock pot and add water. Allow to heat for 30 minutes on high. Meanwhile, brown the beef in cooking oil. Add meat and remainder of ingredients. Allow to cook for 6–8 hours over low heat. Remove stones before serving!

Name: _____

In your best handwriting copy the sentence below.

Never had there been such a feast.
Never had the peasants tasted such
soup. And fancy, made from stones!

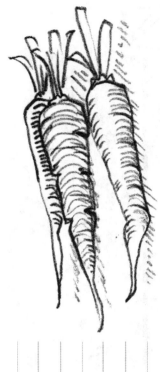

Mr. Putter and Tabby Pour the Tea

CYNTHIA RYLANT

*It is highly recommended
that the following pages
be completed with a toasted
English muffin by your side.*

Name: _____

Answer the questions below using complete sentences.

What did Mr. Putter eat in the mornings?

Why did Mr. Putter want a cat?

Name: _____

Answer the questions below using complete sentences.

Where did Mr. Putter go first when looking for a cat?

_____
_____
_____
_____

Describe Tabby.

_____
_____
_____
_____
_____

Name: _____

Answer the questions below using complete sentences.

Why did Tabby love the tulips?

How did Tabby drink her tea?

What did they do on winter days?

Name:

_____

Draw a picture of Tabby in one of the places she liked to sleep.

Name: _____

In your best handwriting copy the sentence below.

At night each looked for the other as
their eyes were closing. Mr. Putter could
not remember life without Tabby.

Henry and Mudge

Story by Cynthia Rylant

Name: _____

Answer the question below using a complete sentence.

Henry asked his parents for a brother and they said no. He asked his parents if they could live on a different street and they said no. What did Henry's parents say yes to?

Name: _____

Answer the questions below.

List three things Henry said
he did <u>not</u> want in a dog.

Describe Mudge.

Name: _____

Answer the questions below using complete sentences.

Fill in Mudge's statistics.

Weight: _____

Height: _____

Why did Henry no longer worry when he walked to school?

Name: _____

Answer the questions below using complete sentences.

When Mudge walked with Henry to school, what did Henry think about?

What was Mudge's favorite thing?

Name: _____

Draw a picture of two things Mudge loved (other than Henry's bed), then answer the question below using a complete sentence.

Why did Mudge love Henry's bed?

Name: _____

Answer the questions below using complete sentences.

What happened to Mudge when he went on a walk without Henry?

Why was Henry's heart hurt?

Name: _____

Answer the questions below using complete sentences.

How did Henry find Mudge?

Why did Mudge stay close to Henry?

Name: _____

Circle the nouns and underline the adjectives.

Mudge had floppy ears and straight fur.

Mudge loved dirty socks and the stuffed bear.

Mudge smells Henry's lemon hair, milky mouth, soapy ears and chocolate fingers.

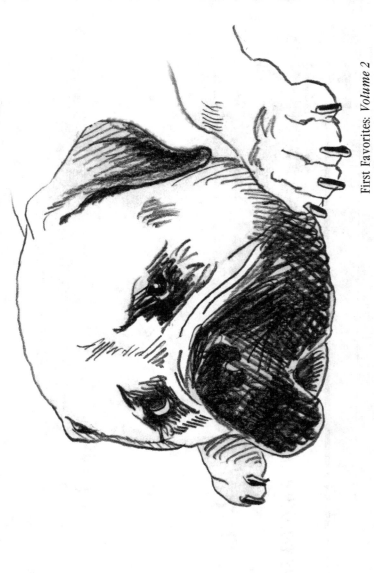

Name: _____

Answer the questions below using complete sentences.

Henry and Mudge were best friends.
They did everything together.

Name: _____

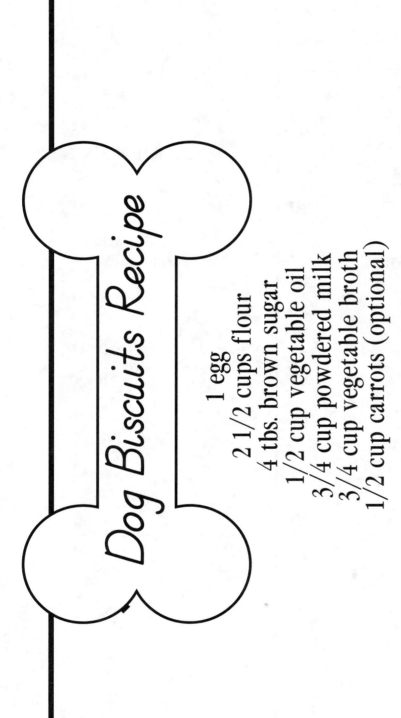

Dog Biscuits Recipe

1 egg
2 1/2 cups flour
4 tbs. brown sugar
1/2 cup vegetable oil
3/4 cup powdered milk
3/4 cup vegetable broth
1/2 cup carrots (optional)

Preheat oven to 300°F. Mix all ingredients into a ball and roll out to about 1/4" thick. Cut with bone-shaped cookie cutter, or strips, or a cutter shape of your own choice. Place on ungreased cookie sheet and bake 30 minutes at 300°F.

Please note, this yummy recipe is only for canine consumption.

LITTLE BEAR &
LITTLE BEAR'S FRIEND

by Else Holmelund Minarik

Name: _____

Answer the questions below using complete sentences.

What is the first thing Mother Bear made for Little Bear to wear?

_____
_____

What else did Mother Bear make Little Bear wear?

_____
_____

Name: _____

Answer the questions below using complete sentences.

Why did Little Bear want
something to wear?

What did Little Bear finally wear after
he put on his hat, coat and snow pants
so that he would not be cold?

Name: _____

Color in the soup ingredients then cut them out
and glue them on a round construction paper "bowl."

I can make soup with...

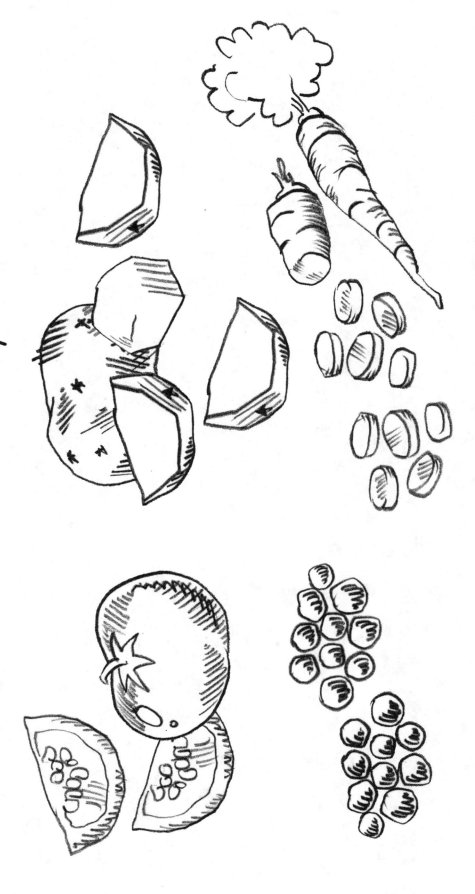

Name: _____

Answer the question below using a complete sentence.

Why did Little Bear make soup?

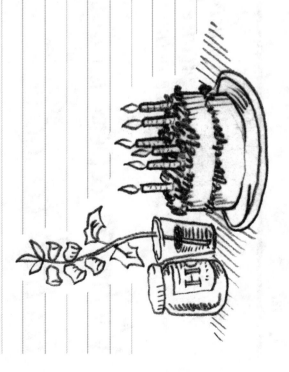

Name: _____

Answer the question below using a complete sentence. Then draw a picture of Little Bear with his space helmet on.

Where does Little Bear want to go?

Name: _____

Answer the questions below using complete sentences.

How does Little Bear think he will get to the moon?

_____

_____

_____

Where does Little Bear really go?

_____

_____

_____

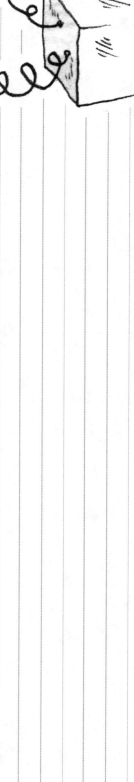

Name: _____

Color in the objects in the squares, cut them out and then paste them on a piece of paper in the order in which they occurred in the story.

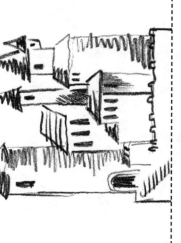

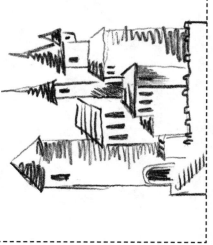

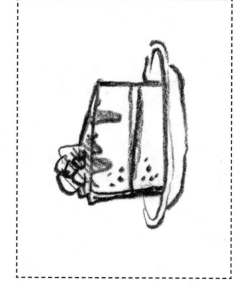

Name: _____

Answer the question below using a complete sentence.

What did Little Bear see when he climbed up the tree?

_____

_____

_____

What did Little Bear see when he climbed down the tree?

_____

_____

_____

Name: _____

Answer the questions below using complete sentences.

What was the little girl's name?

Who did Mother guess Little Bear's friend was?

Name: _____

Answer the question below using a complete sentence.

I was having a party. Who am I?

_____

_____

I went with Little Bear and Emily to

Owl's party. I always go with Emily

everywhere. Who am I?

_____

Name:

Answer the question below using a complete sentence.

I was babysitting ducklings. Who am I?

_____

_____

I got lost in the tall reeds. Who am I?

_____

_____

Name:

Draw a picture of the party at Owl's house.

"Everyone wore a party hat at Owl's house."

Trace the pattern to the right on construction paper, flip the pattern over on the fold line and trace the rest of the hat. Cut out the hat. Color or decorate the hat. Let dry. Curve your hat into a cone shape. Tape or staple closed.

Fold line

Name:

Write a paragraph describing the story "Your Friend, Little Bear."

Name: _____

In your best handwriting, copy the sentence below.

This birthday cake is a surprise for you.
I never did forget your birthday, and I
never will.

AmELia BedElia

BY PEGGY PARRISH

Name: _____

Answer the questions below using complete sentences.

What was the first task that Amelia Bedelia did at her new job?

How did Amelia Bedelia change the towels in the bathroom?

Name: _____

Answer the questions below using complete sentences.

What did Amelia use to dust
the furniture?

_____
_____
_____
_____
_____

How did Amelia put the lights out
when she finished in the living room?

_____
_____
_____
_____
_____

Name: _____

Answer the questions below using complete sentences.

How did Amelia trim the steaks?

Why did Mr. and Mrs. Rogers not care about all the mistakes?

Name:

*Finish the picture using crayons and markers
to dress the chicken like Amelia did.*

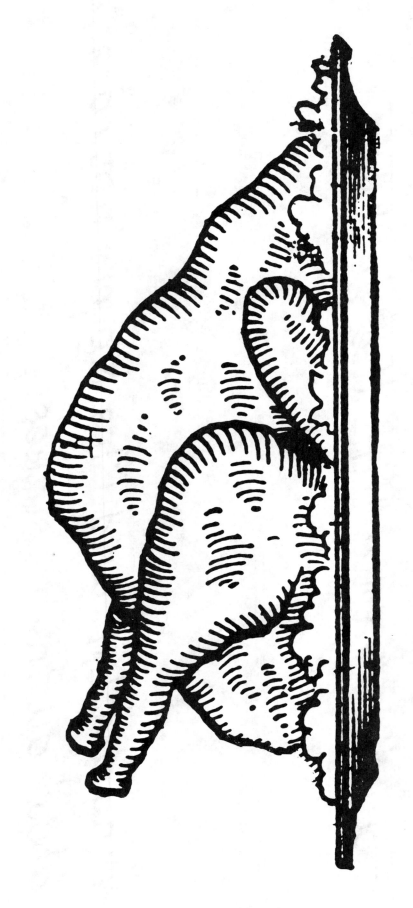

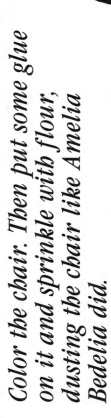

Name: _____

Color the chair. Then put some glue on it and sprinkle with flour, dusting the chair like Amelia Bedelia did.

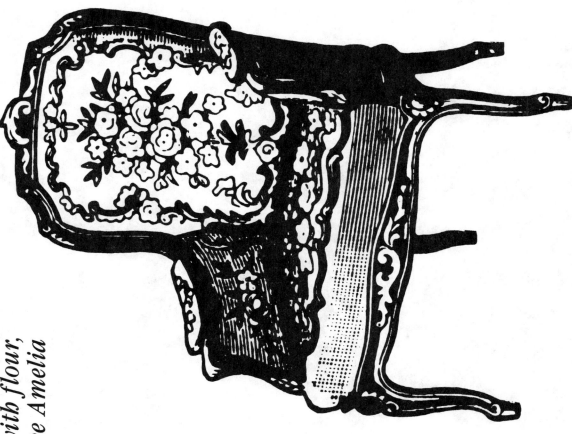

Name: _____

Words and phrases can have more than one meaning.
Draw a picture showing two ways that the phrase
"raining cats and dogs" could be understood.

Name: _____

Draw the drapes like Amelia Bedelia did.

Name: _____

In your best handwriting, copy the sentence below.

These folks do want me to do

funny things.

PETER RABBIT

by Beatrix Potter

Name: _____

My flipsy-flopsy Picture Dictionary

Draw pictures to define the words in each box. Cut out the boxes along the SOLID lines only.

Assemble the pages so they are in alphabetical order after they are folded in the middle. Staple along the dotted spine.

beans

umbrella

Name: _____

basket	wheelbarrow
blackberries	sparrow

Name:

scarecrow	cabbage
radish	garden

Name: _____

cucumber	rake
gate	rabbit

Name:

potato	jacket

Name:

parsley

pie

Name: _____

Answer the questions below using complete sentences.

Where did Mrs. Rabbit forbid her

children to go?

What happened to Mr. Rabbit in

Mr. McGregor's garden?

Name: _____

Answer the questions below using complete sentences.

Where did Peter Rabbit go?

List two events that happened to Peter while escaping from Mr. McGregor.

Name: _____

Color the coat and cut it out to glue onto scarecrow found on the next page.

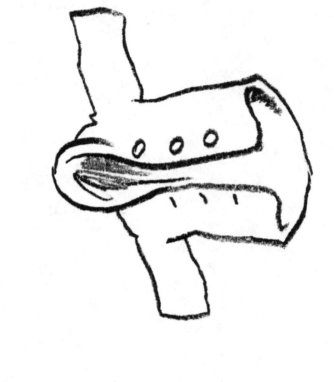

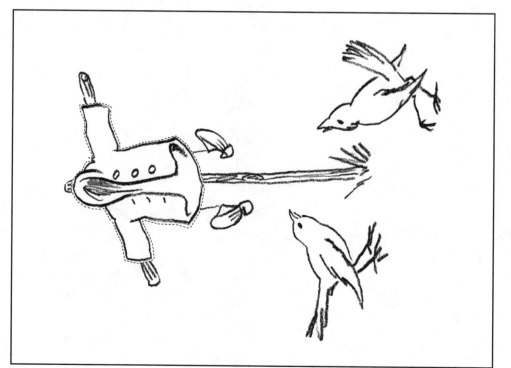

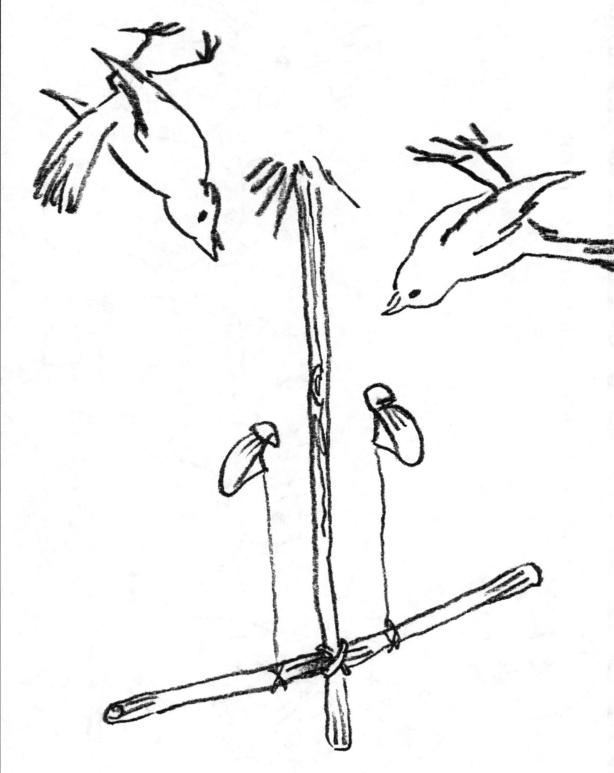

Name: _____

Color the picture and label the characters.

Name:

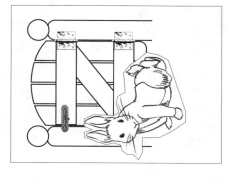

*Color and cut out the picture on this page.
Cut a strip of green construction paper 1" x 8".
Make multiple cuts halfway through the paper
and glue below the fence for grass. Glue Peter coming
under the gate and decorate the rest of the picture.*

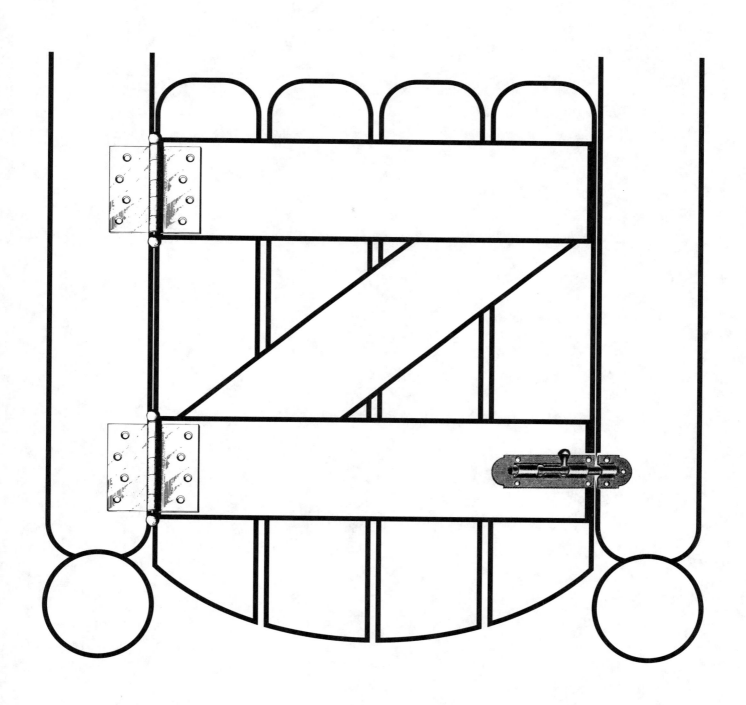

Name: _____

In your best handwriting, copy the sentence below.

Once upon a time there were four little
Rabbits, and their names were—Flopsy,
Mopsy, Cotton-tail, and Peter.

Name: _____

Fill in the blanks.

Mr. Jeremy Fisher lived in a damp house among the _____ .

Mr. Jeremy Fisher loved getting his _____ wet.

Mr. Jeremy Fischer decided to eat _____ for dinner.

Name: _____

Fill in the blanks.

Mr. Jeremy Fisher's boat was
made from a _____ .

Mr. Jeremy Fisher ate a
_____ sandwich.

Instead of a minnow, Mr. Jeremy
Fisher caught _____ .

Name: _____

Fill in the blanks.

Mr. Jeremy Fisher was snapped up by a big, enormous _____.

Mr. Jeremy Fisher and his friends had a _____ for dinner.

Name: _____

Who Am I?

I earn my living by knitting rabbit-wool mittens and muffetees. Who am I?

The scarecrow in Mr. McGregor's garden is wearing my clothes. Who am I?

I believe the proper way to get in a gate is to climb down a pear tree. Who am I?

Name: _____

I caused Peter and Benjamin to sit
underneath a basket for five hours.
Who am I?

I am Little Benjamin Bunny's papa.
Who am I?

Name:

I am a cousin to Flopsy, Mopsy and
Peter. Who am I?

We went out in a gig. Who are we?

I forgave Peter because I was so glad
to see that that he had found his shoes and
coat. Who am I?

Draw a picture in each of the circles to show what mischief the mice caused.

Name: _____

Complete the crossword puzzle by completing the sentences below.

Across

2. The effect of eating too much lettuce is _____ .

3. After eating, the Flopsy bunnies went to _____ .

5. Mr. McGregor put the "leetle rabbits" in a _____ .

6. Benjamin put a _____ over his head.

Down

1. Mrs. _____ saved the bunnies by nibbling a hole.

4. Mrs. McGregor wanted to line her old _____ .

7. Mr. McGregor wanted rabbit _____ .

FIRST FAVORITES COMPREHENSION GUIDE
Answers

MADELINE
Pg. 9
Mice/ice
Light/right
Bed/red
Cry/dry
Hours/flowers
Drank/crank
Habit/rabbit
Light/night

Pg. 10
They should cover the house with vines.

Pg. 11
They should draw three of the items listed below.
Broke their bread
Brushed their teeth
Went to bed
Smiled at the good
Frowned at the bad
Were very sad
Left the house

Pg. 12

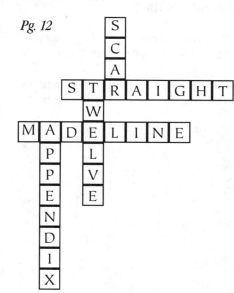

Pg. 13
The children will have different answers; it just needs to be an event that occurred in the book.

NATE THE GREAT
NATE THE GREAT AND THE LOST LIST
Pg. 20
What was Nate the Great?
A detective
What did Nate the Great have for breakfast?
Pancakes

Pg. 21
What did Annie want Nate the Great to find?
A lost picture
Describe Annie.
Annie has brown hair and brown eyes. She smiles a lot.

Pg. 22
Describe the missing picture.
A yellow painting of Annie's dog Fang.
What color did Annie like?
Yellow

Pg. 23
Describe Fang.
He is a big dog, with very big teeth.
Why did Nate dig in Annie's yard?
Because he thought Fang might have buried the missing picture, like he buried his bones.

Pg. 24
Describe Rosamond.
She had black hair and green eyes. And she had cat hair all over her.
What did Rosemond want Nate the Great to find?
Her lost cat

Pg. 25
Where did Nate find Annie's picture?
Harry had it. It was hanging on his wall, and he had painted over it.
How did Nate the Great know that Harry had painted over Annie's picture?
He looked at the paintings on Harry's wall and saw three red pictures and one orange one and realized that Harry painted a red monster over the yellow picture of Fang.

Pg. 26
See page 39 in the book for the example.

Pg. 28
What was the name of Nate's dog?
Sludge
What case did Nate the Great take?
The case of the missing grocery list.

Pg. 29
Why did Rosamond look strange and white?
She was covered with flour.
Why did Nate the Great think Fang took the grocery list?
Because he had a piece of paper in his mouth and Nate thought it could have been the list.

Pg. 30
How did Nate make Fang drop the piece of paper?
He had Sludge bark and that caused Fang to bark.
What paper did Fang have in his mouth?
Nate the Great's map

FIRST FAVORITES COMPREHENSION GUIDE
Answers

Pg. 31
Where did Rosamond get her cat pancake recipe?
She found it near her house.
Where did Nate the Great find the Grocery List?
Rosamond had it, thinking it was a cat pancake recipe.

Pg. 32
I am a busy detective. Nate the Great
I am Nate the Great's dog. Sludge
I drew a map. Nate the Great
I made cat pancakes. Rosamond
I tried to eat the map. Fang
I thought the grocery list was a recipe. Rosamond
I found the missing grocery list. Nate the Great

Pg. 33
The children should draw a map of a familiar place. You may want to go outside to draw the map.

MISS NELSON IS MISSING
Pg. 37
What did the children do when Miss Nelson told them to settle down?
They would not settle down, they whispered and giggled, squirmed and made faces.
When Miss Nelson did not come to school who taught the children?
Miss Viola Swamp

Pg. 38
Describe Miss Viola Swamp.
A woman in an ugly black dress, a real witch
Where had Miss Nelson gone?
Nowhere—she was disguised as Miss Viola Swamp

Pg. 39
doodle
butterfly
shark
paper airplane
giggle
space ship
to-do list

THE BIGGEST BEAR
Pg. 43
Where did Johnny Orchard live?
On a farm
Define humiliated.
reduced to a lower position in one's own eyes or others' eyes

Pg. 44
Why did Johnny always feel humiliated as he walked to the store?
Because as he walked down the road he saw the bear skins on all the other barns, and this reminded him that he did not have one on his barn.
How did Johnny get caught in the bear trap?
His bear was dragging him along and ran right into the bear trap and Johnny went with him.

Pg. 45
Any of the four below is fine.
Maple sugar
Milk
Mash
Apples
Pancakes
Corn
Bacon
Ham
Maple syrup

Pg. 47
That bear of Johnny's is a trial and tribulation to the whole valley. Mr. McLeon and Mr. McCarrol

Better a bear in the orchard than an orchard in the bear. Grandfather

If I ever see a bear I'll shoot him so fast he won't know what hit him. And we'll have the biggest bearskin in the whole valley. Johnny

And I'll always bring him maple sugar. Johnny

He will have a fine place to live, and all he wants to eat. And you can come and see him whenever you want to. Men from the zoo.

It really upsets me when your bear goes through my kitchen shelves. Johnny's mother

Humph. I suppose you know what a bear likes to eat. Grandfather

I like to eat mash, apples, pancakes and maple sugar. Johnny's bear

Pg. 48
:(
:(
:(
:)
:)
:(
:)
:(
:)
:)

First Favorites Comprehension Guide
Answers

A New Coat for Anna
Pg. 53
Why was Anna's mother unable to buy her a new coat?
Because of the war. This caused there to be a shortage of everything.
What idea did Mother have to get Anna a new coat?
She found items to trade with different people to procure the necessary goods to make a coat.

Pg. 54
What was the first thing Anna's mother said they need for a new coat?
Wool
How did Anna and her mother color the wool red?
They died it in lingonberries.

Pg. 55
The tailor said he would be happy to make Anna a new coat. What was the first thing her needed to do?
He had to take Anna's measurements
What did Anna want to do to celebrate Christmas?
She wanted to invite over for a Christmas celebration all the people who helped to make her coat.

Pg. 56
What did Anna's mother make for the celebration?
A Christmas cake

Pg. 57
Farmer and Wool/Gold Watch
Spinner and Yarn/ Lamp
Weaver and Cloth/ Garnet Necklace
Tailor and Coat/ Teapot

Pg. 58
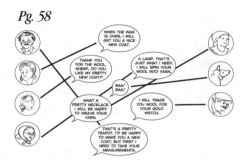

The Emperor's New Clothes
Pg. 65
The answers do not need to be word for word like those below, but should be similar in nature.

The men told the emperor that they were weavers and could weave the most beautiful cloth in the world, that some people cannot see.
The emperor said, "I must have a suit made out of that cloth.

Pg. 67
The emperor gave the men money and gold and silk thread.
The chief ministers told the emperor that the cloth was beautiful.
The emperor looked at the loom and thought I cannot see the cloth.
The two men pretended to work hard on the cloth. They pretended to sew the emperor a new suit.

Pg. 69
The emperor took off his clothes and the two men pretended to help him put his new coat on.
The emperor looked in the mirror and said "My new clothes feel as light as a feather."
Two noblemen were supposed to hold up the ends of the emperor's new cape. They felt around on the floor and pretended to pick it up

In the street people were waiting to see the big parade. When they saw the emperor they said "Look at the emperor! What a beautiful new suit he is wearing."
A little child saw him and said "He hasn't got anything on!"
The emperor thought "The parade must go on so he just kept on going.

Pg. 73
emperor/king
palace/castle
weave/sew
amazing/incredible
shines/radiate
beautiful/pretty
cape/cloak
nobleman/aristocrat

Stone Soup
Pg. 79
water
stones
carrots
beef
milk
soldiers
peasants
pot
stones
cabbage
milk
cider

Pg. 80
Three soldiers trudged down a road.
A large pot was filled with water and three stones.
The peasants added carrots, salt, pepper, cabbage, beef, potatoes, barley and milk to the soup.
They ate and drank and ate and drank.

FIRST FAVORITES COMPREHENSION GUIDE
Answers

MR. PUTTER AND TABBY POUR THE TEA
Pg. 85
What did Mr. Putter eat in the mornings?
English muffins
Why did Mr. Putter want a cat?
He was lonely

Pg. 86
Where did Mr. Putter go first when looking for a cat?
Pet store
Describe Tabby.
Old, cranky tail, orange

Pg. 87
Why did Tabby love the tulips?
she was old and beautiful things meant something more to her
How did Tabby drink her tea?
With cream
What did they do on winter days?
Turned the opera up loud

Pg. 88
The student should draw a picture of the cat either in a bowl, on the mailbox, or in a planter

HENRY AND MUDGE
Pg. 93
Henry asked his parents for a brother and they said no. He asked his parents if they could live on a different street and they said no. What did Henry's parents say yes to?
A dog

Pg. 94
List three things Henry said he did not want in a dog.
Not a short one.
Not a curly one.
And no pointed ears.
Describe Mudge.
He had floppy ears, straight fur, and was short.

Pg. 95
Fill in Mudge's statistics.
Weight: 180 pds.
Height: 3 ft.
Why did Henry no longer worry when he walked to school?
Because Mudge walked with him.

Pg. 96
When Mudge walked with Henry to school, what did Henry think about?
Vanilla ice cream, rain, rocks, and good dreams
What was Mudge's favorite thing?
Henry's bed

Pg. 97
Draw a picture of two things Mudge loved (other than Henry's bed).
The child should draw two things from the following list: dirty socks, the stuffed bear, the fish tank
Why did Mudge love Henry's bed?
Because Henry was in Henry's bed and Mudge loved Henry.

Pg. 98
What happened to Mudge when he went on a walk without Henry?
Mudge got lost.
Why was Henry's heart hurt?
Because he could not find Mudge.

Pg. 99
How did Henry find Mudge?
He went looking for him, calling Mudge' name, till finally Mudge heard him and came running.
Why did Mudge stay close to Henry?
When he slept he dreamt that he was lost again. When he woke up the dream reminded him not to leave Henry.

Pg. 100
Mudge had floppy ears and straight fur.
Mudge loved dirty socks and the stuffed bear
Mudge smells Henry's lemon hair milky mouth soapy ears and chocolate fingers

LITTLE BEAR, & LITTLE BEAR'S FRIEND
Pg. 105
What is the first thing Mother Bear made for Little Bear to wear?
A hat
What else did Mother Bear make Little Bear wear?
A coat

Pg. 106
Why did Little Bear want something to wear?
Because he was cold
What did Little Bear finally wear after he put on his hat, coat and snow pants, so that he would no be cold?
His own fur coat

Pg. 109
Why did Little Bear make soup?
It was his birthday, and he did not see a cake so he decided to make soup in case his friends came by.

Pg. 110
Where does Little Bear want to go?
To the moon

Pg. 111
How does Little Bear think he will get to the moon?
He thinks he will fly.
Where does Little Bear really go?
Tumbling down the hill, till he ends up at his house.

FIRST FAVORITES COMPREHENSION GUIDE
Answers

LITTLE BEAR'S WISH
Pg. 113
Viking boat
Chopsticks
Car
Castle
Cake

LITTLE BEAR AND EMILY
Pg. 115
What did Little Bear see when he climbed up the tree?
He saw the green hills, the river, the blue sea, the tops of trees, his own house, his mother, and two little squirrels.
What did Little Bear see when he climbed down the tree?
Four little birds, a little green worm, and a little girl.

Pg. 116
What was the little girl's name?
Emily
Who did Mother guess Little Bear's new friend was?
The little green worm.

DUCK, BABY SITTER
Pg. 117
I was having a party. Who am I?
Owl
I went with Little Bear and Emily to Owl's party. I always go with Emily everywhere. Who am I?
Lucy

Pg. 118
I was babysitting ducklings. Who am I?
Duck
I got lost in the tall reeds. Who am I?
Little Peep

Pg. 123
Accept anything accurate to the book.

AMELIA BEDELIA
Pg. 127
What was the first task that Amelia Bedelia did at her new job?
She made a lemon-meringue pie.
How did Amelia Bedelia change the towels in the bathroom?
She took scissors and snipped here and there to change them.

Pg. 128
What did Amelia use to dust the furniture?
Dusting powder
How did Amelia put the lights out when she finished in the living room?
She switched off the lights. Then she unscrewed each bulb. Then she hung them up outside on the clothesline.

Pg. 129
How did Amelia trim the steaks?
She got some lace and bits of ribbon and trimmed the steak.
Why did Mr. And Mrs. Rogers not care about all the mistakes?
Because the lemon-meringue pie was so good they forgot all about all the mistakes.

Pg. 130
They should show the chicken with clothes on it.

Pg. 133
1. Show a picture with cats and dogs falling out of the sky.
2. Show a picture with lots and lots of rain drops.

Pg. 134
Draw a picture of drapes on the window.

THE COMPLETE TALES OF PETER RABBIT

THE TALE OF PETER RABBIT
Pg. 145
Where did Mrs. Rabbit forbid her children to go?
Mr. McGregor's garden.
What happened to Mr. Rabbit in Mr. McGregor's garden?
He was put into a pie by Mrs. McGregor.

Pg. 146
Where did Peter Rabbit go?
To Mr. McGregor's garden.
List two events that happened to Peter while escaping from Mr. McGregor.
Chose from two of the events below.
He lost one shoe among the cabbages.
He lost the other shoe among the potatoes.
He ran into a gooseberry net, and got caught by the large button on his jacket.
He was implored by some sparrows to keep running.
Lost his jacket.
Hid in a water can.
Jumped out of a window and upset three plants.
Ran into a cat.

Pg. 150
Mrs. Rabbit, Flopsy, Mopsy, Cottontail, Peter

FIRST FAVORITES COMPREHENSION GUIDE
Answers

THE TALE OF MR. JEREMY FISHER
Pg. 156
Mr. Jeremy Fisher lived in a damp house among the _____.
Buttercups
Mr. Jeremy Fisher loved getting his _____ wet.
Feet
Mr. Jeremy Fischer decided to eat _____ for dinner.
Minnows

Pg. 157
Mr. Jeremy Fisher's boat was made from a _____.
Lily leaf
Mr. Jeremy Fisher ate a _____ sandwich.
Butterfly
Instead of a minnow, Mr. Jeremy Fisher caught _____.
Little Jack Sharp the stickleback

Pg. 158
Mr. Jeremy Fisher was snapped up by a big enormous _____.
Trout
Mr. Jeremy Fisher and his friends had a _____ for dinner.
Roasted grasshopper

THE TALE OF BENJAMIN BUNNY
Pg. 159
I earn my living by knitting rabbit-wool mittens and muffetees. Who am I?
Old Mrs. Rabbit
The scarecrow in Mr. McGregor's garden is wearing my clothes. Who am I?
Peter Rabbit
I believe the proper way to get in a gate is to climb down a pear tree. Who am I?
Little Benjamin Bunny

Pg. 160
I caused Peter and Benjamin to sit underneath a basket for five hours. Who am I?
The cat
I am Little Benjamin Bunny's papa. Who am I?
Old Mr. Benjamin Bunny

Pg. 161
I am a cousin to Flopsy, Mopsy and Peter. Who am I?
Little Benjamin Bunny
We went out in a gig. Who are we?
Mr. And Mrs. McGregor
I forgave Peter because I was so glad to see that he had found his shoes and coat. Who am I?
Peter's mother

THE TALE OF TWO BAD MICE
Pg. 162
The pictures should be any of the following:
Chopping at the ham with a knife/ broke a plate/ break the ham/ broke the pudding, lobsters, and fruit/ threw clothes out the window/ stole the bolster/ stole a chair, a bookcase, a bird cage, and a cradle/

THE TALE OF THE FLOPSY BUNNIES
Pg. 163